GRIEF

GRIEF

Difficult Times—Simple Steps

Emily Lane Waszak

ACCELERATED DEVELOPMENT

A member of the Taylor & Francis Group

USA	Publishing Office:	ACCELERATED DEVELOPMENT
		A member of the Taylor & Francis Group
		1101 Vermont Avenue, N.W., Suite 200
		Washington, DC 20005-3521
		Tel: (202) 289-2174
		Fax: (202) 289-3665
	Distribution Center:	ACCELERATED DEVELOPMENT
		A member of the Taylor & Francis Group
		1900 Frost Road, Suite 101
		Bristol, PA 19007-1598
		Tel: (215) 785-5800
		Fax: (215) 785-5515
UK		Taylor & Francis Ltd.
		1 Gunpowder Square
		London EC4A 3DE
		Tel: 171 583 0490
		Fax: 171 583 0581

GRIEF: Difficult Times—Simple Steps

1 2 3 4 5 6 7 8 9 0   B R B R   9 8 7

This book was set in Times Roman. The editor was Cindy Long. Cover design by Michelle Fleitz.

A CIP catalog record for this book is available from the British Library.
∞ The paper in this publication meets the requirements of the ANSI Standard Z39.48-1984 (Permanence of Paper)

Library of Congress Cataloging-in-Publication Data

Waszak, Emily Lane.
  Grief: difficult times, simple steps/Emily Lane Waszak.
    p. cm.
  Includes index.

  1. Bereavement—Psychological aspects. 2. Grief. 3. Death—Psychological aspects. I. Title.
BF575.G7W36   1997
155.9'37—dc21

                                                    97-3857
                                                    CIP

ISBN 1-56032-657-3 (paper)

This book is dedicated to my family and to my fantastic husband for all of their love and support.

This is also dedicated to all of the survivors out there. Together, we can make it.

CONTENTS

WHY THIS BOOK
WAS WRITTEN

Death has been around for as long as life, yet no one really knows how to deal with death and everything that accompanies it when it occurs in each of our lives. This fact is not a mystery, and it should not be a taboo subject. Instead, we need to learn the techniques necessary to assist others in coping with the death of a loved one. After we master these simple steps, we must educate others so that death becomes a little more familiar and maybe even a little easier to deal with.

Peace and Comfort,

ELW

WHAT TO SAY

1

Say "I'm sorry."

Let's begin with the basics, and the most basic of it all is this two-word phrase. It's comforting, it's simple, and no more needs to be said, especially if you are uncomfortable and unsure of what to say. It's short and easy to remember, it offers sympathy, and it allows you to say that you are suffering as well. No other words need to accompany this phrase.

It's ironic, though, that people see "I'm sorry" as cliché or overused. Not so. It's true that many people offer their condolences with this phrase over and over again to the survivors. However, when was the last time you heard of someone getting upset because someone expressed his or her sorrow in this way? No survivor will tire of hearing someone extend his or her sympathies during a period of grief.

2

Do not say, "It's for the best."

The deceased may have suffered from a traumatic injury or a lengthy illness, and he or she may have been absolutely miserable during the last days, but for you to point that out is not of any comfort. In fact, it is quite disturbing. Even when we know that it is best that suffering is over for the deceased, the pain of the loss is just beginning for the survivor. Often, the survivor does not see that this "is for the best" and can become resentful of those who feel this way. We all feel we know what is best for us, but what is best for one person is not necessarily best for another. While you may feel relief that the suffering is over, the survivor might not. My grandfather died after an eight-week stay in the hospital. I knew that I was glad that he was no longer in pain, and I knew that it was better this way, but that was for me to decide. I found myself growing resentful of others who would tell me that it was a relief. Who were they to tell me how I should feel?

If, however, the *survivor* states that "it's for the best," it is perfectly acceptable to agree. The survivor may be able to tell you that he or she feels this is for the best, and that it is good that the suffering has ended, but let the survivor say that. Do not assume that he or she feels this way.

You do not want to remind the survivor that the deceased suffered either. As the individual is dealing with the death, and the grief that accompanies it, he or she does not want to think about the pain and suffering of the final days of the deceased. Unpleasant memories are better left untouched. If you feel lost for words and you want to say something, bring up a pleasant memory, maybe one from the final day, one that is peaceful and calming. But do not feel that you have to say anything. You are being supportive just by being there for the survivor.

3

Say, "I care about you."

Say this, but be sure to say it with meaning. When the person knows that you care, it comforts and soothes. Survivors need to know that someone cares, that they can turn to someone for a hug or a smile or just quality quiet time to relax and let go. "Care" is such a calming, healing word, and it provides a warm feeling.

When the survivor is dealing with the rough times of grief, he or she may feel alone and become depressed. This is a very emotional and overwhelming period, and support is a crucial element to keep the survivor going. There is so much support in your caring for the survivor and his or her family, and it is essential that you reinforce your support, understanding, and care throughout the grieving period.

You may feel that these phrases are corny or rehearsed, but believe me, these phrases are effective guidelines for you to use and build on. Use the phrases to assist you in preparing what you want to say and in feeling comfortable with others when dealing with the death of a loved one. Nothing nice ever can be repeated too often. Become comfortable with these basics, and use them for your foundation for grief assistance in the future.

4

Say, "I love you."

If you love someone, let him or her know. While this is true at any time in life, it is *necessary* after someone suffers a loss. People need to know that they are loved, and nothing eases their grief more than being surrounded by love.

Sometimes there is a great deal of guilt involved with love when a death occurs. Often, survivors wish that they could say "I love you" to the deceased "just one final time." To hear the words from someone else is comforting, and it may help reduce the empty feelings resulting from the loss. Hearing the words also gives survivors the opportunity to reciprocate the emotion.

On the other hand, a survivor may not be able to open up to you and display the love that he or she may feel. Be prepared to be turned away. Remember that the survivor has just lost someone special, someone that he or she loved, and to lose that love is so difficult. It is also difficult to open up his or her heart to love again, love that could be snatched away so quickly and so unfairly as it has with this death.

Do not be discouraged with this. Give your love unconditionally and, with or without a response, offer your love to the grieving survivor. This is when he or she will need it most.

5

Say, "I'm here to listen."

This may be the single most important phrase in this book. Listening is so critical, but this means *listen*—not interpret, criticize, or add anecdotes throughout the individual's story. This is the individual's time; let the person utilize it however desired, and listen.

Remember also that if you say it, mean it. Believe me, the individual will take you up on this—if not immediately, then later. There will come a time that the person will need to unload, and it may become extremely emotional. On the other hand, the individual may ease into disclosing feelings. The person may make mention on occasion of memories, and though these may come across as light comments, take them seriously and respond accordingly.

When talking to children, you may want to pursue this differently. Questioning and drawing the child out generally is more effective than just listening. Ask children to tell you how they feel, what they miss most about the deceased, and what makes them feel better when they are sad. Be ready for any response from a child; those little minds are filled with big ideas. It is amazing what they can come up with when given the chance to share their feelings.

You will see this idea appear in many other suggestions throughout this book because listening is important and so critical. Remember, "listening" means exactly that—to *listen*, not interpret, criticize, or add anecdotes throughout the survivor's story.

Allow time to sit and listen, uninterrupted, to the entire story and to the survivor's feelings. Do not take this time to compare or share your stories of loss with the survivor unless, of course, he or she asks you to. We all have our stories to tell, our feelings to share, and our solutions to provide. Think back to a time when you needed someone to talk to, and you were attempting to tell your story and the other person kept jumping in with how he or she felt and what he or she went through—something the individual felt was similar to your story. Wasn't it frustrating? Didn't you just want to say, "Shut up and let me finish! What I need now is a friend to listen and not a problem-solver to tell me how to fix this!"? Of course, most people will not say this and they go on, eventually finishing what they had to say but leaving without the sense of solace for which they had come searching.

6

Do not give unsolicited advice.

This goes hand in hand with the previous suggestion. The survivor wants to talk and wants you to listen. That is it, unless you are told differently. The individual wants to grieve, and that means working through feelings and emotions and thoughts that are all his or her own. There are so many thoughts racing through the survivor's head already, and the last thing he or she wants to hear is how to feel or what to feel. You even could offer ideas that were not there before, leading to greater confusion and inner conflict for the survivor. Why cause a problem? Just keep your mouth closed and let the survivor open up without the fear of being criticized, analyzed, or advised.

If the individual asks for advice, be careful with the advice you offer. Do not be harsh, critical, or judgmental. Tread lightly on the emotions and feelings that the survivor may be experiencing. The survivor is coming to you as a friend, as a support system, and if you diminish the importance of his or her confiding in you with your own criticisms, you are shutting the survivor out and making the individual feel unimportant and uncared for. This also may damage the individual's self-esteem.

You will see this idea repeated often in this book—be supportive. Focus on the positive, and reinforce the positive at every opportunity. This is what the survivor needs most.

7

> ## Tell survivors what a wonderful person the deceased was.

Focus on the positive. If you are nervous about this and you do not know quite what to say, practice! Sit down and make a list of the deceased's good traits, and then expand that list to include why each of the traits was good. How did the deceased use these traits? Was there a great smile that greeted people each day? Was there a contagious laugh that livened up any event? What about a strong work ethic? Did the deceased work hard and stick to commitments until the job was completed? There are so many things that you can look for and easily find.

But a list may just be an outline for you. Sometimes we not only need a script, but we need to rehearse it. At home or even in the car on your way to visit the survivor, practice what you want to say. Talk out loud until you feel comfortable, or take a small tape recorder with you and listen to yourself. See what you think works and what you think does not. By the time you are on the spot, the words most likely will flow out of you and you will not feel intimidated or embarrassed or worried that you might say the wrong thing. When you talk about good traits and focus on the positive, there isn't anything that is the "wrong thing" to say.

Be cautious, however, and do not overdo it by being so complementary that you sound fake. You do not want to insult the survivor by sounding like you are forcing yourself to come up with memories or creating stories that appear to be too much. Be honest and be positive. By being yourself, you will come out looking great and being helpful.

8

Share happy memories.

You can go back to the previous suggestion to get ideas for preparing for this. Begin thinking about good times you have shared with the deceased and the survivors. There always is another story to be told, and there always are laughs to be had with these stories. You may want to use these stories to entertain others who also are visiting the survivor. This takes some pressure off of the survivor, and it allows others to jump in and share their happy memories as well.

Another nice idea is to buy a journal and write down some of your fondest memories of time spent with the deceased. Share this with or even give it to the survivor. This is a wonderful tribute to the deceased, a tribute that includes the best memories and good times. The survivor will be able to reread the stories at his or her convenience, and it will be a nice item to hand down through generations. This is especially nice for a person who has lost a spouse and has children. When the initial wave of grief passes and life gets back on track for the family, this will comfort them when they gather and read it together. For small children, it will be a perfect way to learn about their mother or father.

9

Do not remind survivors
of the deceased's faults.

Remember to focus on the positive. Nobody wants to hear about the time the deceased drank too much and acted like a jerk. People need positive reinforcement at a time of grief. People need to find a reason to smile and laugh and remember the happy times, not groan and grunt about the awful times. None of us are perfect, and we all have our faults, but none of us want to be remembered for those faults, right? Resist bringing up negative stories.

Remember that if you do have negative stories, others may not be aware of them. If you share these stories, they may only create unsettling feelings and possible resentment toward you. This also may give the survivor a story or memory that he or she would rather not know. Be selective and share the positive and only the positive.

10

> ## Do not say, "It's all in God's plan." Survivors cannot help but wonder how God could "plan" that kind of hurt.

Even if you strongly believe that God (or any other deity) has the "master plan" for all of our lives, survivors do not want to hear that during a time of grief. Sometimes the *survivor* will make this comment, and it is fine to reinforce his or her thoughts, but do not offer this comment on your own accord. No one wants to think that God wanted to take such a special person away; no one wants to believe that God caused such hurt.

Most of us never sit down and write out a plan that is destructive or that will hurt others, so imagine what a survivor feels like when you offer "God's plan" as an explanation. This is like telling the survivor that God set out to hurt him or her intentionally, and the individual will wonder what he or she did so wrong to deserve this.

You do not have to offer an explanation to the survivor of why the deceased died, so do not take it upon yourself to come up with an answer. There are no answers. There is only support and love and comfort that you are able to give effectively without stirring up hard feelings. If you give these elements and these elements alone, you will be in perfect shape when assisting the survivor throughout the grieving process.

11

Say, "I know it's a difficult time for you."

This is not a deep statement or one that you have to make an effort to mean what you are saying. A death is a difficult time, and everyone recognizes that. By letting the survivor know that you recognize this, you are relating to the survivor; you are letting him or her know that you understand the significance of this tragedy and how painful this must be.

12

Do not avoid the survivors because you do not know what to say.

Avoidance is worse than saying something you feel sounds stupid. If you make a conscious effort to avoid the survivor, he or she will notice and will begin to feel like something is wrong. The individual needs your support.

Throughout this book you will find plenty of suggestions of what to say or what to do if you are self-conscious about saying the wrong thing.

13

In the case of a painful and lengthy illness, be cautious of the phrase, "I'm glad that he [she] is no longer suffering."

While we generally are relieved when a loved one is no longer suffering, it is difficult to rejoice in death. Yet quite often people will offer this phrase as a condolence to the survivor with good intentions. I am just as guilty as anyone else for using this phrase, but I realized when the tables were turned and the phrase was used on me that it really is not as much of a comfort as I once thought. On the one hand, I agreed, and I was glad that the deceased was no longer suffering from the pain and agony that he had experienced for so long. To hear it from someone else, however, was not as comforting as I once had thought it would be. When *I* would say to someone else that I felt relieved that the suffering was over and they would agree, I felt better. They were reinforcing my feelings, not telling me how to feel. This is a very sensitive issue, and you need to use caution. Be careful not to tell the survivor how to feel, but go ahead and support his or her feelings and thoughts when these are shared with you.

I think that many survivors stir up feelings of hurt when this is brought up by someone else. It is a terrible time watching a loved one suffer and not being able to do anything about it. It is horrible to see a loved one ache, not be able to communicate, slowly lose control of his or her body, get frustrated with not being able to do things he or she once was able to do, or lose total sense of where he or she is, who he or she is, or who the surrounding loved ones are. To hear someone say that the suffering is over conjures up images of the suffering all over again, and it possibly may cause feelings of guilt as well. No, there was nothing the survivor could have done to put the deceased out of his or her misery, but believe me, the survivor wishes there had been. The survivor most likely thought many times that he or she wanted to end the loved one's pain, and it is natural to feel badly about being unable to do that. Just remember to tread lightly in this area when speaking to the survivor, and reassure him or her that his or her support and love comforted the deceased in the final days.

14

Say, "You look great."

People tend to feel ragged and run down after dealing with a death. Reassure the individual that he or she looks great, looks calm, and looks like he or she is keeping it together. The survivor needs to be built up and comforted. If indeed the survivor is looking really run down and exhausted, offer to answer the phone or greet people at his or her home while he or she takes a nap. This will allow the individual to attempt to take a little rest without jumping up each time the phone or doorbell rings. Or, if you are able, treat the survivor to a make-over, haircut, or massage to relax a little. Then tell the survivor how great he or she looks. If you feel good, you radiate that outward and you look good. Let the survivor feel good and gain a little extra confidence.

15

Say, "You've been so strong for your family."

Encourage and then offer to let the individual be weak for a while with you. The survivor cannot be a pillar of strength 100% of the time. It will not work. This only will make the individual grow more and more tired until he or she collapses from the exhaustion of acting strong. Reinforce the strength that the individual has exhibited, but allow him or her to be weak and unwind with you. Reassure the individual that he or she can cry, yell, and be angry and that does not make the individual a failure for not pulling the strong act. It makes the individual human. Sometimes we lose that element and we try to be superhuman when dealing with trauma. We are not superhuman, though, and we must remember that.

16

Say, "It's perfectly all right to let it all out."

Survivors sometimes feel that they are supposed to keep it all inside when in front of others. No one wants to appear weak or needy, but everyone needs to let out their emotions. Crying in the shower so that no one knows you have done so is not healthy. Parents sometimes feel that they should not grieve in front of children when the truth is quite the contrary. Children should be included in the grieving process. If a child sees a parent cry, it validates the child's feelings and tells him or her that it is perfectly normal to cry, express confusion, or relate his or her own sadness in front of the parent. Children need to feel that they are allowed to talk about their feelings, and adults need to listen.

17

> ## Then offer, "I can listen to you when you are ready to talk about this."

Offer this to both adults and children. Adults need to know that they have an outlet to go to when they feel the need to open up and finally discuss everything. Sometimes it can take months before a survivor feels comfortable opening up about his or her feelings. The survivor also may be experiencing avoidance and denial. Give the individual time to come around and open up.

Children, however, generally want to open up and let it out as soon as possible. Do not overlook or underestimate children. They are very observant and quite insightful, and you may find that the thoughts and feelings of a child actually are comforting to you or to others. Give surviving children the opportunity to speak and open up. Believe me, you will be glad that you did.

18

> # Do not say, "Buck up. You have to get on with your life eventually."

Some people take a day off of work, return the next, and go on as normal. This individual may still go to his or her softball league, attend PTA meetings, or follow his or her normal routine. For some, the sooner normalcy resumes, the better. Others, however, need to take a leave of absence from work. Maybe the survivor needs time away from the daily routine, the meetings, the social events. This is acceptable for short-term, but the individual may need reinforcement to return to life as it used to be. Others may go on but feel the need to visit the grave daily or look at photo albums each night. This is not abnormal or an action that should be discouraged so long as other activities continue. If a mother wants to visit the grave of her daughter every night after work, let her do it. But if she wants to sit at the grave all day every day, this is cause for concern.

Support the grieving process for the individual, but attempt to help reestablish the everyday routine that was in place prior to the death so that the survivor can carry on as before. If the survivor was spending every day caring for the deceased through an illness, try to find a new routine that suits the survivor. If you belong to a social group or athletic team, encourage the survivor to get involved. Even if you establish a routine for only every Wednesday evening, it is a start, and it will assist in mainstreaming the individual back into society and into life.

Do not be the one to decide what is normal, though, as this must be determined by the survivor. Your encouragement will be appreciated, however, and the survivor will need your support.

19

Never say, "Get over it."

There is no statement more cruel than this. You do not "get over it" and "move on" as if it were a tennis tournament that you just lost. This is a life that was taken from the survivor, and the void never will be filled. Survivors do not get over a death. Yes, it gets easier with time, and yes, life does go on for the survivors, but the rate at which normalcy begins to return to day-to-day life is dependent upon the individual.

Your support and encouragement, and not your advice to "get over it," is what the survivor needs. The survivor will resent you for making this statement, and you will appear negative and unfeeling. Keep in mind that what may be normal to you may not be normal to the survivor. Be patient and try to understand what is normal to the individual, and assist him or her in attaining that standard of living.

20

Do not monopolize the conversation with stories of your previous losses.

If you feel that your story may be helpful, use it, but do not monopolize the conversation. The survivor needs to talk. Once when I was in this situation, I went for a ride with a survivor who had lost his sister very recently. As he drove, I mentioned that I understood to a point how he felt, that he had to be strong and hide his emotions because he was the oldest sibling (and now an only child), and how he felt that his parents would have a difficult time if they saw his "weakness." I had felt that way before too. I also mentioned that I had lost a sister. I said all of this in about three sentences in a minute and a half, that's all. He began asking me questions, and I answered them, but this also led to his opening up and discussing how he felt. He saw that I was able to relate to him, to his feelings, and he felt "normal" again. He had found someone who could understand what he was going through. Notice I did not carry on with my experiences or my feelings or endless stories of losses I had experienced. I related to him using one recollection, and this led to an afternoon of discussion where he was able to open up and I was able to listen.

21

Do share your pain and your feelings of loss for the deceased.

You do not have to feel the same strong emotions that the survivor is experiencing to be able to relate to the pain of the death you both have experienced. Share your sadness and emotions with the survivor. You may present a different perspective to the survivor as well. The survivor may be missing so many qualities of the deceased, and your mentioning a particular aspect may allow the survivor to focus on something he or she may not have thought of before. Maybe you miss the deceased's ability to tell a joke, or shoot a basketball, or his or her contagious laugh. The survivor enjoys hearing about these things that you will miss. It not only reminds the individual of a good quality of the deceased, but it also makes the survivor feel good that you have a warm feeling about the deceased, that you can relate to missing those features. It may remind the survivor of a trait that he or she may have overlooked.

22

Never tell the survivor how to feel.

Feelings and emotions are personal, and no one can tell another how he or he should feel. Survivors feel many emotions throughout the grief process, and this is confusing enough without being told how or what to feel.

Instead, reinforce the feelings that the survivor is experiencing. Validate his or her emotions, and respect what he or she is going through. Nothing is more encouraging than hearing from others that the survivor is dealing with normal feelings. The survivor has enough to worry about without thinking that he or she is abnormal.

23

Do not judge or criticize.

Once you begin to judge or criticize, you begin to push the survivor away from you. The individual will feel the negative energy, and he or she will run in the other direction. Negativity is the last thing this person needs. Instead, be supportive and encouraging.

If you find yourself being critical, get yourself a journal and track your feelings. You may find that you are having difficulty dealing with the death, and the reality may be that you want the survivor to finish his or her grieving so that you are able to. Keep track of your thoughts and emotions. Perhaps if you see a destructive pattern that the survivor is exhibiting, then you could approach the individual with your concerns. Address these concerns one by one as you have written them down, but do this as a concerned friend, not a judgmental critic.

HELPFUL THINGS TO DO

24

Offer to take the survivor to a movie, to dinner, or just out for a drive.

Just get out of there! The survivor has been through so much: funeral preparations, hosting friends and family, entertaining family for the duration of the planning and funeral, taking care of kids, cooking, cleaning, all of the other day-to-day activities, and all the while grieving over his or her loss. The survivor feels like a mountain of burdens have been placed on his or her shoulders, but he or she is unable to let it show. The survivor is supposed to be strong, together, and calm through it all, and by the time the funeral is over, he or she needs to get away and try to relax by just escaping.

Maybe there is a good movie showing. Maybe you know of the survivor's favorite restaurant. Maybe you know of a place special to that person to which you could drive and relax such as a river or a hill or a nearby park. Help the survivor get away from it all and not worry about visiting family, phone calls, or people stopping by. While people mean well and want to help, there comes a point when a survivor needs a little space to breathe and a little uninterrupted time of his or her own.

You know the survivor, and you know what he or she enjoys doing. Plan something pleasant and relaxing for the survivor depending on his or her tastes. If you feel that the survivor would enjoy an evening at home more than going out, then rent a movie, order a pizza, take a board game over, and spend the evening in. The survivor will appreciate the effort you make and the time you spend.

25

Send a sympathy card.

If you do not know what to say and you are uncomfortable facing the survivor, purchase a card that helps express how you feel. You do not have to add any additional verbiage if you do not wish to; simply sign your name and send it. This does two different things: it makes you feel better, and it consoles the survivor. A survivor never can receive too many cards, and you do not have to worry about saying the wrong thing. Card stores now offer such a wide selection of sympathy cards, and you can find one that will say exactly what you want to say in a very comforting manner.

It is truly amazing what a card can do for a person. You might think that it is not that big of a deal since "everyone" sends one, but not everyone really does. Oh, they mean to, and they think about it, but so many people do not get around to it. Those who do, however, brighten even the darkest day. The survivor will appreciate a caring, thoughtful card. After I went through a tough death and a tremendous amount of grief, a friend gave me a card that was so touching and warm. To this day, I still have that card. When I feel down or lonely, I take a look at the card and it reminds me that someone cares. Sending a card is a simple gesture that will continue to provide warm and caring memories for the survivor.

26

Make a dinner and share it
with the family of the deceased.

The last thing an adult survivor wants to deal with is making dinner for the family and the out-of-town guests who may be visiting. Whip up a casserole or something that can be reheated easily or served cold and take it to the home of the survivor. This is a very thoughtful gesture immediately following the death, and it is also a nice idea a week or two later after all of the commotion has ceased and the survivor is left alone. Weeks after the funeral, the survivor may feel burned out and need that little bit of help.

If you do not feel that you have a talent for cooking or you are not sure what to prepare, there are plenty of other options. Go to a local grocery store with a deli and purchase a tray of cold cuts and cheeses and a loaf of bread. Or buy a salad sampler with a variety of options. If you have a friend who is a great cook, ask him or her to help you prepare something special for the family. Finally, if you live in an area that offers a food delivery service, purchase a gift certificate for the survivor. Some restaurants offer their own delivery as well. If you know of a favorite restaurant of the survivor that will deliver, purchase a gift certificate there.

These suggestions may sound simple, but the survivor will be exhausted from all the activity. Your elimination of even the most minor worries from the survivor's life during the immediate days following the death will be more than appreciated.

27

Offer to help with the funeral arrangements.

This is a traumatic time filled with emotion and confusion. It is difficult to think clearly or organize thoughts. Many people go into overdrive and just go through the motions. For people who never have been through the making of funeral arrangements before, it becomes increasingly confusing. If you are able to help with this, please offer. Go to the funeral home and assist the survivor with the final plans. Funeral directors are well-trained, and they generally are very good at what they do; however, they may not know the survivor personally, and you do. You may even know what the wishes of the deceased were. You also may remember the minor details that the survivor may overlook.

If you are involved with someone who is suffering from a terminal illness and you want to be prepared, call a local funeral home and ask the director for a tour of the facility. Take other family members with you if you wish. I toured a funeral home with a group, and it was the most educational experience I ever have had on the steps that must be taken from the moment the person dies until the person is buried. I feel that it is important for everyone to be aware of this so that each person knows what to expect, what decisions need to be made, and how to handle the arrangements before the time comes. It is so much easier to go through the motions of something familiar than to be trained on something new during such a traumatic time. Funeral directors are there to help you; consider getting the help before you actually need it. You will be glad that you did.

28

Help write thank-you cards.

Writing thank-you cards is time consuming and emotional, and any additional help generally is appreciated. It could make for a nice afternoon to sit down with the survivor and write out thank-yous. This provides companionship for the survivor while accomplishing work that needs to be done. Often It is much easier to write notes with a friend than to sit alone and not know where to start. Thank-you notes generally are written within a relatively short time of the funeral, and this is usually a time of confusion and exhaustion for the survivor. Make it as little work as possible for the survivor.

The sooner that thank-you cards are sent, the better. Speaking from an etiquette point of view, these need to go out quickly. Speaking from an emotional point of view, the survivor will have one less thing on his or her mind once these are sent, and it becomes one less item to worry about on the to-do list. Some survivors may not even think of this task, and if you suggest that this be done and then offer to help with the writing, the survivor will feel gratitude toward you.

29

Send a "thinking of you" card
a couple of weeks after the funeral.

After the death has occurred, friends and family rally around the survivor and express regrets. These same people are there for the funeral, which is generally within a week of the death. But after the funeral is over and things settle down, everyone else returns home and life goes on as before the death. The survivor still feels the loss, though, and needs support. A nice gesture is to send a card two or three weeks after the funeral to let him or her know that he or she is in your thoughts. Cards are amazing because they are small gestures that mean so much. First of all, people love to get mail. It is nice to open your mailbox and see something addressed to you (other than junk mail addressed to "Occupant"), right? Of course it is, especially when you see that it is a greeting card. The survivor even may think that it is a belated sympathy card, and imagine his or her pleasure when a "thinking of you" card is there. What an inspiration to a survivor who is feeling a little down. You do not even have to write a lot inside; just the thought that you were thinking of the survivor is enough to brighten his or her day.

30

Share a smile.

A smile says so much with so little effort. A smile warms; it says that you care, you understand, you sympathize, and you are there if the survivor needs you. The smile is the universal symbol of peace, joy, and happiness. A smile cannot go wrong. Think about what you do when someone smiles at you. How do you feel? If you are in a bad mood, does it make you cheer up even just a little bit? If you already feel good, does it make you feel better? Of course it does. Even during the darkest moments of this grieving period, if you offer a smile, you more than likely will receive one in return and you will make the mood just a little brighter.

31

Light a candle in memory of the deceased on special occasions.

When planning a special dinner or family gathering, survivors may want to light a candle as a symbol of the deceased. Candles are peaceful and serene and, for many people, the soft glow of candlelight is relaxing and soothing. You may want to encourage a younger child (not too young, though) to light the candle and maybe another to blow it out at the end of the event. Get the entire family involved. You even may want to go a step further and after lighting the candle, go around the table and each read a prepared saying (religious or inspirational) or share a memory with respect to the deceased. This may be difficult the first few times, but it is a wonderful tribute and a nice way to tie in the deceased with the family during a special dinner or event. This also gets the subject out in the open right away; no one is sitting through dinner feeling emotional over the loss and the fact that the deceased is not there to share the special day with the family. This may be customized to your particular situation, and with some creativity, this may be pleasurable and even something the family looks forward to at each gathering. You even may find that the family creates special candle holders decorated for each holiday to house the memory candle.

32

Create a photo album of the deceased and give it to the family.

Gather favorite photos and arrange them in a nice album or as a collage for the family. This is just like a wedding album or a baby book; it is a piece of family history that is warm and loving. The deceased was important in the survivors' lives, and remembering is a happy event. This is a remembrance album, something to turn to when one wants to remember or introduce the deceased to another person, perhaps a new member of the family. This is a beautiful memorial for the family.

33

Create a video from home video clips or photographs and share it with the family.

Videos are fun. You could create a video from other video clips and/or from photos. This gives life to the person who has died. You are able to see the individual walking and talking and laughing, maybe celebrating a birthday or winning a race. There are so many options here, and the ideas are endless. It is a living tribute to a person who has died. Visit a video artist and ask for ideas on this. You will be amazed with the options; this can be set to music or designed in a personal way that will be cherished by all.

34

Buy memorial flowers for the deceased's church and dedicate a service to him or her.

Most churches offer this opportunity to members. Buy flowers that remind you of the deceased. Let the family choose the flowers if you wish. Another nice option is to, after the service, have the flowers delivered to the family or to a member of the church who may be hospitalized or convalescing at home. It will brighten his or her day, and it will make you feel good. Some churches will arrange for members to receive the flowers, or you can arrange to deliver them yourself to the hospital or home. You could take the flowers to a retirement or senior citizen center so that they can use the flowers to decorate for a function. Recycle the flowers, and let as many people enjoy them as possible.

35

Ask, "Is there anything I can do to help?"

Do not take "no" for an answer. Most people will tell you out of courtesy that they do not need help; others may actually take you up on your offer. Make sure you turn the "no" people into "yes" people so that you are able to help. If there is a lot of family coming into town or if everyone has just left, offer to help clean the house. The survivor will be exhausted and will need the extra help whether he or she realizes it or not. There are many suggestions on how to help included on these pages, and you can come up with your own in addition to these. You know the survivor and what he or she will need most, so offer your services. You may be needed simply as a friend who is available to listen.

If the survivor is a single woman (especially a woman who has just lost a husband), she may be uncomfortable sleeping alone in her house. You could offer to stay with her or have her stay with you, even if she has children. She could be a little nervous or up-tight about being alone (or being the only adult in the home), and she really will appreciate your thoughtfulness.

A single man who has lost a wife may feel that it is not masculine to want to have someone else around, but do offer. If you see hesitation when he refuses, push a little and let him know that it is perfectly acceptable to not want to be alone. You may find that he comes around and accepts the company after all.

36

Offer lots of hugs.

Hugs are one of the best inventions I can think of. They are warm, cuddly and a way of relaying so much with so little effort. In one motion, they say, "I care, I am here, I support you." Give hugs very generously not only at a time of grief but always. This way, when a survivor is grieving, he or she knows by your hug history that you care and are there to be a support.

If you visit the funeral home and are comfortable in doing so, offer hugs to the family and friends of the family of the deceased, even people who you do not know. The individual is suffering and will appreciate the gesture of kindness that you are extending.

37

Offer to help clean the deceased's room and pack up the deceased's belongings for storage.

The survivor may want to do this alone, but many times the individual would love for someone to help out with this difficult task. It is easier to go through a room full of reminders with someone else, and if you do this, be prepared to laugh and cry. There will be some great reminders in there, and it even can be kind of fun to go through another person's life. Different items will trigger many memories, and it can be enjoyable if you go in with an open mind and do not expect this to be only somber and sad.

38

Rent a comedy and watch it with the survivor.

Maybe you know an actor who is the survivor's favorite, or maybe you know what type of comedy will entertain the individual. Rent a comedy video or two, get some soda, pop the popcorn, and you are in business. Sit back, relax, and enjoy a good "night out," an escape from the sadness and emotions. It is nice to just curl up at home in comfortable clothes and not worry about getting all fixed up to go out, especially when going through a tough time. This is an opportunity to laugh and enjoy an evening, probably something the survivor has not done in a while. He or she will appreciate your thoughtfulness and care.

39

**Buy a daily calendar with inspiring quotes
or whimsical notions to pick up
the survivor's spirits one day at a time.**

Sometimes even something so simple can make a person's day. It is wonderful to start the day with an upbeat one-liner that can carry a person through the day. It gives the survivor a reason to get out of bed, a reason to go on with the day rather than hole-up and feel bad. I have seen a variety of calendars, and you will be able to find one that is personal and suitable for the survivor. There are many types including religious, whimsical, motivational, inspirational, meditational, those that deal with angels, and so on. You even may find one with a character or topic that the survivor really enjoys. This does not necessarily have to be inspirational; it can be fun, but be sure to customize this to complement the personality of the survivor.

40

> ## If the deceased is cremated, help the survivor find a nice place to spread the deceased's ashes. Accompany the individual (if he or she desires) when the individual spreads or buries the ashes.

The location may be chosen already. In some instances, however, the survivor may need assistance in finding a proper location and will be helped if you offer suggestions with regard to places the deceased enjoyed visiting or spending time. Maybe there is a favorite hunting spot or tree or park. Maybe the ashes are going to be buried in a memorial garden or cemetery. Once the location is determined, the survivor may appreciate your accompanying him or her to distribute or bury the ashes.

It is acceptable for the entire family to take part in this. You may want to encourage the survivor to make a day of it. Pack a picnic or go for a drive and reminisce about the fun times with the deceased. If there are small children involved, maybe they would like to draw pictures or write notes to the deceased and place them with the ashes. Each family member could place a rose on the ashes and share a happy memory as they do so. Instead of getting all worked up over an emotional day, make it more enjoyable and relaxing by creating a pleasant atmosphere.

41

> ## When a family member dies, let the survivors take something that reminds them of that person from the deceased's home if possible.

An individual may want to have a little memento that means something special to him or her. When I was young, my great-grandmother had several little figurines and knickknacks, but there was one in particular that made me think of her. It was a heart-shaped tin with a sandalwood-scented candle in it. The scent always has made me think of days spent with her. When she died, I asked if I could have that tin with the little bit of candle still in it, and to this day I have it sitting out on a shelf in my home. Sometimes when I feel down or lonely, I will hold that heart in my hand and open it to inhale the aroma that makes me feel so good. It is wonderful for someone to be able to have that kind of memory with something so little and meaningless to anyone else. If you are in the position to allow surviving family members into the deceased's home to take a memento as a reminder, by all means allow them to do so. This opportunity may give them happy memories for years to come.

If you are not in the position to do this but you are interested in an item from the deceased's home, ask a survivor if it is acceptable for you to take that particular item. Chances are good that the survivor will be more than willing to let you do so, especially if it is something so meaningful to you.

42

**If given the opportunity to keep a memento
of the deceased, do not fight over an object
with someone else. It only will leave you
with bitter memories.**

If you find yourself in the situation where you want a particular
item that another survivor wants, try to negotiate. If it has a specific meaning to you, explain that to the other person and try to
reach an agreement. If you must, though, try to kindly give the
item to the other survivor and find a suitable replacement. I know
that this may be difficult, but think of the consequences. Is this
item really worth destroying a relationship over? Is it worth having
hard feelings with another family member over? Would the deceased
want you to fight over this and injure the relations that you and the
other survivors share? The deceased probably would not want that
to happen after he or she has died; out of respect for the deceased,
make an attempt to resolve this peacefully.

Death can cause many damaging blows to relations in families
due to the arguments and hard feelings that occur when more than
one person wants one object. Think about this; these are only objects. Family and love run so much deeper than objects. Objects
can be replaced; families cannot. It is important to keep this in mind.

43

**After a long day at the funeral, play
your favorite music and take a long,
soothing, uninterrupted bath.**

Relaxation and your own personal time is important, especially following such a long and emotional day. Find some time to give to yourself, and run a long, hot bath, turn off the lights, light candles, turn on your favorite soft music, whip up a hot cup of tea or cocoa, and lock yourself in the bathroom after telling others that you need an hour to yourself and that they need to respect your request.

If you have another form of relaxation that you prefer, by all means do that instead. This is just a suggested guideline. The point is that you need to do something for yourself; spend some relaxing time doing something that you enjoy. Go into your room and read a good book, or go for a drive in the country. After all you have done for everyone else, you now need to take some time out for you.

44

> # Find ways to help the survivor around the house. Do not tell the survivor, "Call if you need anything."

Instead, think of specifics and ask if you can help with those things. It is easier for survivors to accept specific favors than to call and ask for your help. The survivor more than likely never will call to ask for your assistance. Shovel the driveway in the morning, mow the lawn, trim the hedges, bake a meal and deliver it as the survivor is arriving home at the end of the day. There are so many little extras that you can do that will mean much to the survivor.

45

Buy helium balloons and take them to the cemetery.

Take helium balloons, strips of paper with a hole punched near the end of each one, crayons, markers, pens, pencils, glue, and glitter with you to the cemetery. Give everyone a strip of paper and instruct them to write a message to the deceased with words, decorations, or both. An individual could write a poem, create a design, write a message, or create whatever he or she desires. When everyone has completed their strip of paper, tie each strip to a separate balloon. Stand all together, each holding a balloon with his or her own message, and release the balloons together. You may prefer to go around and have each person read what he or she wrote or explain what the pictures mean. It is nice to share, but do not force anyone to disclose if he or she is uncomfortable doing so. After you release the balloons, watch them gracefully float away into the peaceful blue sky. Watch for as long as you like, and see in what direction the balloons move. This activity can become very emotional for some, as this is a very personal event. It can be a beautiful tribute to the deceased and a special time for everyone involved.

46

Create a memory blanket or quilt
for the survivor; it is warm, is secure,
and is a tangible memorial. Even
a manufactured blanket with your
personal touch added is nice.

The survivor can do many things with a memory blanket. He or she can display it on a quilt rack, pack it away as an heirloom, or use it personally. If it is displayed, the survivor and others can view it often and be reminded of the special person that it represents. If it is packed away and handed down throughout the years, there will be a story along with it and hopefully some pictures to pass down to future generations so that the memory of this wonderful person will live on. Or finally, the survivor may want to keep the blanket handy and curl up in it to feel closer to the deceased when feeling down and alone. There are many possibilities with this, and it is a touching gesture for the survivor.

Many shopping malls house shops that will personalize afghans, quilts, and blankets. You can be creative and have a tasteful tribute to the deceased customized for the survivor.

47

Volunteer to watch the children of a survivor for a few hours to allow the individual to have time to be alone.

The survivor with children will need time to be alone. Children are just that—children. They are full of energy, and a grieving parent may not have the same level of energy to keep up with their needs and demands. If you are able, volunteer to watch the children for a few hours. You could give the survivor a gift certificate to a spa, the theater, a restaurant, or another local event if you prefer, or you could take the children out and let the survivor have the house to himself or herself. Many activities are available for children including movie matinees, a children's museum, a zoo, a park, and a nature walk. Make it an adventure, and have fun.

The adult survivor may be reluctant to let you do this for many reasons. The survivor may have anxiety about being away from the children so soon after the death, or the survivor might not want to burden you with the children. Remember, the survivor probably is fatigued, and the children may seem to the adult to be extremely hyper and energetic. Be convincing, and talk the survivor into having some time alone. Be sure to reinforce the fact that letting the children go is not a selfish act, that the adult is not "dumping" the children on you, and that the survivor can be assured that you *want* to do this. After the survivor has had time alone, he or she will be very thankful for that time and for your allowing him or her to have it.

48

Send a copy of the obituary to the survivor in a "thinking of you" card.

This may sound tacky, but survivors many times want to keep a copy of the obituary for a scrapbook or a family history that has been or will be compiled. Some survivors want to send copies to out-of-town relatives who were unable to attend the funeral. If you enclose the obituary in a "thinking of you" card, it is a thoughtful gesture and not a tacky one. Think about the times that you do clip items and send them to friends and family such as birth announcements, engagements, wedding announcements, employment announcements, and articles of interest. Obituaries are no different. They are clippings of family or friends who we want to acknowledge. This is a nice gesture and worth the effort.

DEALING WITH THE
DEATH OF A CHILD

49

Do not minimize the loss of an unborn child.

A loss is a loss. It does not matter how far along the mother was in the pregnancy. It does not matter if the baby would have been unhealthy, impaired, or disabled. That was the child of two people, two people who looked forward to the arrival of a new family member, a new little someone to love. Suddenly the plan has changed, and this baby never will sleep in the cradle in the nursery that was decorated just for this baby. Mom or Dad never will rock this baby in the new rocking chair. The baby will not open his or her first gifts this Christmas.

People grieve the loss of an unborn child in different manners. To some, the matter is done and over and let's just move on. They do not want to talk about it, think about it, or acknowledge it in any way. This may last forever, or the survivors may begin grieving years later. But do not assume that the silent person is not grieving. Perhaps they are, but all emotions are on the internal back burner so that you may not see an outward display of grief. The survivor hurts but masks his or her hurt by denying that it is there. That is his or her way of "dealing" with it.

In other instances, the survivor may be grieving outwardly, and you may witness tears, frustration, and anger. The survivor, especially a mother, may be going through feelings of guilt, believing that it is her fault that the child died. Did she eat the wrong foods? Exercise too much? Lift something too heavy? Mothers wonder what they have done wrong and what could have prevented this. Fathers may feel the guilt while wondering if they allowed their wives to do too much (e.g., laundry, housework, or continuing with a job).

And even though it is nobody's fault, the guilt remains and the hurt intensifies. This is when the couple needs family and friends the most. The reality of it is that the baby probably was going to die regardless of anything that the mother or father did. There was something else wrong with the baby. The mother and father need to be loved and comforted and reassured that the death was not their fault.

You may encounter a couple where the two partners feel drastically different from one other about the same situation. One wants to grieve while the other wants to put it behind him or her. It is important to feel out the situation, see how the survivor feels, and comfort accordingly. It is never inappropriate to acknowledge the loss by extending your sympathies. This is typically an uncomfortable situation for most of us. You cannot discuss the deceased because you have no memories to share, and this limits conversation. Do not let this hinder you from comforting a survivor. A major component in assisting someone through this situation is to just be there. Let the survivor talk, and let him or her talk about anything he or she wants. Chances are there are a lot more topics on his or her mind than the death. Let the individual open up, and you may find that he or she wants to talk about anything other than the deceased child.

50

Do not say, "At least you're young; you can try again."

This is not a basketball game that can be replayed tomorrow; this is a loss, a death of a family member, and it is a tragic and sorrowful time. Age has nothing to do with how the couple feels, and "trying again" sounds like a situation where the cook made a dish that didn't turn out and he or she can simply start over from scratch. The fact is that the couple lost a child who they were looking forward to. This baby was stripped away from them, taken from their lives. They may not know where to go from here. This grief also can cause a strain on even the best of marriages, and the couple needs support from those around them. If prior to this incident you would get together and play cards every Thursday night, continue to do that. Do not deviate from normal activities. And do not be afraid to ask how the couple is doing. This is not a taboo subject, and avoidance may make the couple feel uncomfortable. Chances are they want life to go back to normal as quickly as possible while at the same time being able to grieve.

Be sure to be there for both of the parents and not just the mother. While the mother most likely will be the one to outwardly grieve while the husband will tend to mask or even deny his feelings, both parents need your encouragement and support.

51

> # Do not say, "God must have needed a little angel up there."

While the child may have been an angel to the couple, the family does not want to think that God chose their child to be taken away from them. The family may be questioning why God would take such a wonderful child away, just strip the baby out of their lives. A need for an angel is not a worthy reason for a child to die in the minds of these parents. The parents may resent your suggesting that God needed an angel there while they needed that same angel in their home and in their own lives.

Actually, it is not appropriate for you to offer an explanation of any kind to the parents. No reason will be good enough for them. Instead, offer comfort. Be a support system and a friend who will listen.

If you feel that you want to give a gift to represent their loss, consider purchasing an angel. Angels and babies go hand in hand for many people. Often angels and babies are both perceived by people as beautiful, comforting, and innocent. Angels also are very popular; there is a great variety of shapes and sizes of angel gifts that can be chosen from when looking for an angel gift for the parents.

52

> # Following a miscarriage, never say, "At least you didn't know the child; you weren't attached yet."

The parents were attached; the baby was the child who they were planning for, talking to, bragging about, and building a loving relationship with. Once the parents learned that they were expecting, the attachment began. The two adults became parents-to-be from the moment the pregnancy test was positive. The planning began, and the excitement grew with each moment.

The sex of the child may have already been determined, and the child may have had a name already chosen. The parents may have decorated a nursery for the baby. This is a painful reminder when they pass the room each day. Each time a friend asks how the pregnancy is coming along, the mother or father has to explain and stir up the emotions all over again. The parents have to call their parents and other family members who were anticipating the birth and tell each one what has happened. As mentioned previously, the mother also may experience feelings of guilt and failure because she "lost" the child.

Also, many decisions need to be made. If the pregnancy was advanced, does the couple decide to have a funeral? Does the couple try to get pregnant again? If so, how soon? What are the chances of another miscarriage? How quickly do you announce another pregnancy to friends and family? These questions may occupy the thoughts of the couple.

This is another instance where you do not want to avoid the topic of the baby. Ask the couple how they are holding up. Invite them over for dinner to get them out of the house and into a fun activity. The couple needs friends to support them.

53

> ## Remember that a miscarriage is still the death of a child; the parents and family are suffering.

Too often, people downplay the loss of an unborn child. The couple may be told that this was not really a child who they knew, but in truth they *did* know this child. This baby had grown inside its mother for some time, the two parents possibly feeling the kicks and turns of the fetus, listening to the heartbeat, and looking forward to the child's arrival. The child may have had a name. The unborn child became a part of the family the day he or she was conceived, and the child was accepted from the day the parents realized that they were expecting. The loss is as significant as any other loss, and it is important to recognize and treat it as such.

Remember too that the entire family is experiencing a loss. There are grandparents who were looking forward to a new grandchild, aunts and uncles who anticipated a niece or nephew, and sisters and brothers preparing for a new sibling. Loss through a miscarriage is not just something that parents go through. There is disappointment for each family member and friend, and all seem to feel a sense of loss.

54

When a child dies, do not say, "At least you have your other children."

Other children are not going to replace a void left by a deceased child. That is like telling a widow that it is a good thing there are other eligible men out there for her to date; that will not comfort her in the loss of a spouse. When a child dies, there is a great deal of tension and stress put on a family. Parents may blame themselves or each other, siblings do not know how to react, and the family is in turmoil. Remember that just because there are other family members, that does not diminish the significance of the loss the family is experiencing.

Try to assist the family in their grief and help them deal with what will be one of the toughest experiences a family can go through. The family may have other friends too, but they need you to be there at this time. One friend does not make up for others just as another child does not make up for one that has died. The family needs a great deal of support and love, and any effort you can make will be appreciated.

55

> # When a baby dies, do not say, "It's too bad you only had the baby for a short time."

The parents most likely are glad to have had the child for the time they did even if they question why they only had the child for a short time. If you say to the parents, "It's too bad you only had the baby for a short time," it may be taken as you saying that they should never have had the child for any time, that the child would have been better off dying before the parents "got to know" him or her. Parents are very sensitive after the loss of a baby, and they do not want to be reminded of how they only had the child for such a short time.

56

Do not say, "At least you had a chance to know the baby."

No time is ever enough, and the parents most likely will be sensitive about this. Even though the mom and dad may have had time to learn about the infant's habits and distinguish the baby's cries, no parent ever will feel that he or she had enough time with the baby. This perfect little addition to the family was ripped away from their arms and torn from their hearts, and that kind of pain is difficult to comfort.

Reassure the parent(s) that you understand that this must be troublesome and painful. Let the parents know that it is acceptable to feel hurt, disappointed, confused, and angry. Also assure them that this death was no fault of their own or the siblings. Again, there may be an overwhelming amount of guilt associated with the death.

SIDS, or Sudden Infant Death Syndrome, is a mysterious disease. The infant (usually under the age of 12 months) dies unexpectedly, typically while sleeping. There is no explanation, no warning, and no symptom, and imagine the horror to enter a nursery and find that a baby whom you presume is sleeping has died. A parent may feel that he or she should have checked on the baby earlier, or there may be a number of "should haves" on the part of the parent. Many areas have support groups for parents and families who have experienced a death related to SIDS. Strongly encourage the family to attend sessions so that they may find solace in discussing it with others who have gone through the same or similar experiences.

57

> ## Do not offer the assumption that the baby probably had something wrong with him or her anyway.

Even if this is the case, no one wants to be told this. The parents may take this as you telling them that they did something wrong, that the death is their own fault. There also may be another issue along that line—the parents could be blaming themselves or each other—and this sort of statement will make a tense situation worse. The parents may resent you and feel that you are placing blame on them and that there was something wrong that they themselves should have noticed.

58

Let the parents know that you hurt, too, and that it does not seem fair.

Reinforce their feelings. No, this does not seem fair. Yes, it hurts immensely. Think about this. How many times have you been reading about a child who has died—maybe in an obituary of a child in the newspaper—and once you noticed the age, you immediately scanned to find the cause of death, how many siblings are surviving, and so on? You automatically feel for the parents who are dealing with so much. This hurts a great deal to see, and this is someone whom you have never met. It is natural to hurt for others, and when the injured party is a friend or relative, the aching intensifies. It is perfectly fine to relate your pain, anger, and confusion to the parents, and it will show them that you understand that they have these same feelings. It validates their feelings.

59

Children suffer the miscarriage of a sibling. Ask them how they feel.

Siblings generally are overlooked when there is a miscarriage in the family. Older children may understand that the baby has died, but they usually are not encouraged to discuss how they are feeling about this. The topic becomes forbidden in their minds because Mom and Dad do not discuss it or ask the children how they are feeling. The children grow up with a hurt inside that they feel they are not supposed to discuss. More confusing, though, is when a miscarriage occurs and smaller children are not told. All of the sudden there is no baby, Mom is not pregnant, and no explanation accompanies the situation. The "baby in Mommy's tummy" is a topic that is dropped, causing confusion for children. Even the youngest of children have questions, but many are afraid to ask these questions because no on else in the family is discussing the topic.

If you are a parent who has experienced a miscarriage, explain this to your children. If you find that it is too difficult for you to do, ask a friend or family member to help you. It will clear the air and assist children in understanding the situation.

HELPING CHILDREN COPE WITH DEATH

60

Children need guidance and reassurance when death affects their lives.

Children of any age need help in coping with a death. Believe it or not, children as young as three years old understand the trauma of death. I have heard the most profound words come from the mouths of three- to six-year-olds who are dealing with a death in the family. Are you surprised? You may be, but let me explain why you may not have realized this previously. Children are the ones who are overlooked in these types of situations. Adults tend to focus on the older children and other adults, believing that young children do not understand or can't relate to the events around them. This is so false. Young children do not talk or share their feelings about it because they do not think that they are supposed to. Death is taboo. If it were a topic open for discussion, they would be asked about it. Children do understand and they do need to talk about their feelings and thoughts on death. They may have a lot of questions as well. Ask them to talk to you, and give them the opportunity to openly discuss the death and ask questions.

61

Give a child the book *The Fall of Freddie the Leaf* by Leo Buscaglia.

Read *The Fall of Freddie the Leaf* (L. Buscaglia, 1982, Thorofare, NJ: Charles B. Slack Co.) together and discuss it. Adults and children alike will learn something from this interesting look at death.

This book provides an accurate but delicate way to look at death without scaring a child. It is a beautiful book, and it may open the door to questions that are on the child's mind. Children are curious by nature, and they want to know everything about anything. Have a frank discussion as you read this book and honestly answer questions that pop up along the way. Offer information as well if you feel comfortable doing so. Death is an uncomfortable subject for almost everyone, and children really know how to put adults on the spot unintentionally. Be ready for anything when engaging in a conversation with a child.

62

Do not be afraid to answer children's questions about death.

There are no *wrong* answers, provided you are open and honest. If you hide something, the child will see right through you and may have a difficult time trusting you or believing any of the other answers that you give. If you are honest, a child will look to you as a trusted adult and a friend who will not let him or her down.

You also can be honest by explaining that you do not know some of the answers about death. You do not know what it feels like, but you can tell the child how you think it might feel. Ask the child how he or she thinks it feels. Ask the child to answer the same questions that you are asked. What color would you make death? What would it taste like? What would it smell like? Get creative and feel out the child's perspectives on the topic. You do not have to possess all the answers; you just need to be open, honest, and available to discuss this when the child feels the need to. Be prepared for questions to pop up out of the blue. Death may preoccupy the child's mind for a while. This is normal. Children are fascinated with new things, and death may be newly introduced to the child. You can make the conversation interesting, educational, and maybe even fun. Remain calm, keep relaxed, and be honest— these are the keys.

63

> ## There are three reasons a person dies: The individual is very, very, very sick; very, very, very old; or very, very, very hurt.

Share these three reasons with the child. By accentuating the "very," you diminish the thought that the child will die from a broken bone or the flu. Death is very scary to a child, especially if it is the first death that the child has experienced. All of the sudden someone is gone, and the child is told that the deceased never is coming back. Certainly there are going to be a lot of questions and curiosities about this. Be honest. Explain what you are able to convey accurately to the child. Tell the child that Grandpa had cancer, and explain what cancer is and what it does to a person. If someone is in an automobile accident, explain this, but also reassure the child that riding in a car does not mean that you are going to die. This is when you need to reinforce the "very, very, very hurt" to the child.

In the case of a suicide, the child should be told the truth, but the "truth" can vary with age. This depends on the maturity of the child more so than the chronological age. With a small child under the age of five, you should be truthful that the deceased killed himself or herself, but there is no need to go into graphic detail. The child may ask how this happened, and you can provide a basic description without a lot of detail. Expect this to come up again, though. As the child ages and asks for more detail, give that detail to the child. Honesty is the best policy, and a child will be able to handle the truth. If you lie now, the child eventually will discover the truth and may resent the fact that you previously covered up the truth.

64

Allow the child to touch the corpse, but do not force the issue.

Children are curious creatures, and they like to use their senses to the fullest to absorb a situation. Many times, a child will want to touch a corpse but is afraid that he or she will get into trouble. Reassure the child that it is acceptable to touch the body. Consider walking up to the casket with the child to be there for support. This is a scary time. The child also may be anxious and fear that the body will sit up and grab at his or her arm like in the horror stories or movies that he or she may have read or seen.

Also, do not get upset if the child seems to have fun with this. He or she may laugh out of nervousness or run to a sibling or cousin to tell that he or she has touched the body. This is a normal reaction.

Be prepared for a lot of questions or comments regarding this situation. The child may want to talk about how the body looks or feels. Be open and honest, and do not avoid the topic. The child will feel better if you are open to discussing this.

65

Take children to the funeral.

Many parents have difficulty deciding whether or not to take children to the funeral. I firmly believe that the best answer is to take the children and let them experience a funeral. Again, there will be questions and comments, but at least the child will see first-hand what is involved in a funeral. If you leave a child at home, he or she will wonder what is going on at the funeral and why he or she could not go. This will bring up a lot of questions and misperceptions. The child may think of funerals as scary. The funeral becomes something unknown to the child, and that is the most frightening feeling. Include children as much as possible. If you experience a death of someone who was not really close to the child, this may be a good opportunity for you. Take the child along to this funeral and he or she will see what is going on without a great deal of emotion, or less emotion possibly than a close friend or family member.

66

**Make arrangements with the funeral director
to give children a tour of the funeral home;
let the director answer questions that
may be tough for you.**

This could be done a couple different ways. One, you could do this before a death is experienced to introduce children to death. Another way is to arrange for a tour earlier in the day before the family visitation time. Let children walk around with the director and see the visitation rooms, the casket room, the offices, and so on. Let the children direct questions to the funeral director. This will take some of the stress and uncomfortable feelings away from you. Do not think that this as ducking your responsibilities; think of it as utilizing the funeral director for what he or she is trained to do—explain and comfort. It will not be emotional for the funeral director whereas it may be for you, and the children will get a good education.

67

Never lie to a child about death.

If you lie to a child about death, the child eventually will find out the truth and will resent the fact that you lied or covered up the truth of a death. Children have so many questions that need to be answered. You are the adult whom the child is coming to in his or her time of need. If you are dishonest, the child will no longer know whom to trust. As mentioned earlier, you do not have to be graphic or brutal with your honesty and you can disclose what is age-appropriate, but be honest. The child needs this, especially at a time such as this.

68

Use the words "died," "death," and "dying" when talking about death.

To say someone is "gone," that he or she "went away," that you "lost" the person, or that "God took the person away from us" only confuses and frightens children. "Gone" could be thought of as thrown out in the trash. "Lost" could be like a toy in the backyard or a dog that ran away. Lost also implies that the deceased may be coming back some day. The child also could associate lost with the local store and expect that with an announcement of a lost person that the deceased will walk up to the front of the store and meet the family. People who lose things find things, and the child will want to find the deceased. Imagine, too, what will go through the child's mind the next time that he or she is lost. "God taking the person" also could be frightening. The child will wonder how God decides whom to take and when to take them. The child could experience anxiety that he or she will be chosen at any time or that another family member may be taken away. There is no need to scare a child when you can be honest and explain to the best of your knowledge what has happened while using proper terminology.

69

> # Take the time to talk to the other children when a sibling has died. They have strong feelings too.

Children in a family where there is a miscarriage are confused and often do not know what they are supposed to do, what they are supposed to say, or how they are supposed to feel. They need to talk and open up, and they need someone to listen to them. Children often are overlooked as adults feel that adults need the friendship and attention. Children will not necessarily volunteer the information to you if you do not approach them. Ask the child how he or she feels. Ask what the child is going through. Ask the child to tell you what hurts the most, what he or she misses the most, and what makes the individual feel better.

No child is too young to talk. I have talked to three-year-old children who have been so profound and intellectual in how they have looked at, questioned, and answered the situation that I have been amazed. The reason we do not hear more of this is because we forget to ask them the questions. We assume that they are too young to understand, and we push them aside and deal only with the adults. Make this all-inclusive and talk to children of all ages. They are in need of your time and attention.

70

Buy a teenager who has lost a parent the book *Tiger Eyes* by Judy Blume.

Tiger Eyes (J. Blume, 1981, New York: Macmillan Children's Group) is an excellent book dealing with the untimely death of a parent. A teenage girl experiences the death of her father and the many issues that surround the experience. A teenager or even a pre-teen truly will appreciate this book. Blume is an outstanding author, and her look at the subject of death and grief is accurate and touching. You, too, may want to read the book to see a teenager's point of view about death, relocation, and continuing on with life. Blume has successfully captured the emotions and realities faced by a person who has lost a parent. The book will provide you with a deeper understanding and appreciation of the situation.

71

Rent the movie "Charlotte's Web."

"Charlotte's Web" is a wonderful movie and a superb tool for explaining death to a child. It even helps adults understand death a little bit more. This classic tale shows the life cycle in a straightforward but soft fashion. Because "Charlotte's Web" is a cartoon geared toward children, a child can view the movie and get a better understanding of death without being terrified. There are many opportunities for the child to question events in the movie, and it would be nice for a parent to watch this with the child to clarify any confusion that might arise. Again, this movie is straightforward, but when dealing with death, children are bound to come up with a variety of questions or comments. If necessary, watch the movie more than once with the child. As with any movie, people notice things the second time that they might not have the first.

72

To prepare a child before a death is experienced, buy the child a goldfish.

If you dread the moment when you will have to explain death to a child, prepare the child before the time arrives. Purchase a goldfish. When it dies, the child will grieve and ask questions, and these questions may be easier to answer about a fish than if you wait until a family member dies. While a child will be sad because of the death of the goldfish, the child is not attached as he or she would be to a relative, a friend, or even a dog or cat. A goldfish is a pet that has a short life, is not cuddly, and does not have a specific personality and traits that form an emotional attachment within the child. This is an easier way to deal with death without a great deal of emotion. You will be able to answer questions and discuss the topic much easier than if you were dealing with a personal loss of your own.

73

Avoid euphemisms with children. Use simple language that a child will understand.

Be straightforward with a child and use language that is simple but sincere. Use the following words: death, died, sick, cancer, tumor, car accident, hurt, etc. Children do understand these terms, and you can explain them further if need be. Do not tell a child that Grandma went to sleep and did not wake up, or that cousin Timmy got an "owie" and died. The child will perhaps never again want to go to sleep or do anything that could hurt. Be open to discussion and be honest. Children want to know the real terminology, the real causes of death, and the real emotions that you are feeling because of a death. You can be honest without being too graphic.

74

Spend a day doing arts and crafts with children. The adult survivors may want to get involved too.

This is a nice way to get everyone's mind off of the death and focus on something fun and creative. Pick an upcoming holiday or find a craft that you are particularly talented at making and share this with the children. You can do it for fun, or you can make grave decorations or memory decorations for the children to hang in their rooms to remember the deceased. Look through children's craft books or use the Internet to search for unique ideas.

If you are not a real artsy-craftsy type of person, whip up a batch of cookie dough or buy some premade dough. Get out an assortment of cookie cutters, buy a variety of frostings and decorations, and spend the day baking and decorating cookies. You and the children could deliver the cookies to other survivors. The children will enjoy it, and it will divert their attention from the grief to a fun activity, even if only for a short time.

The idea here is to get the children involved. Children need a healthy, creative outlet, and by using a little imagination, you can come up with the perfect activity for them.

DURING HOLIDAYS
AND ANNIVERSARIES

75

Do not forget the deceased during the holidays; the family will not.

Do not pretend that the deceased never existed. It is not inappropriate to ask the survivor how he or she is feeling about the upcoming holiday. Ask if it feels lonely or if it is a difficult time. Ask what you can do to make it a little easier. Maybe just spending time with the survivor will help.

The holidays can be very emotional and depressing for many people anyway; thus, more suicides occur between Thanksgiving and Christmas than any other time of the year. I think it is because people feel so lonely. If a death has occurred, the depression becomes much worse. Keep this in mind as November rolls around.

If the survivor you are dealing with is elderly and recently has lost a spouse, make an effort to spend time with him or her. If you live a long distance from the survivor, call and write. Just keep in touch to let him or her know that you care. Imagine being married 30, 40, or even 50 years and then losing that person who accompanied you all of those years. How lonely! Many senior citizens feel lost and confused, and just do not know where to go or what to do. Also, a great deal of alcoholism exists among senior citizens, and it seems that many drink out of boredom and loneliness.

If you are able to visit, do so often, and include the survivor in your holiday plans including gift opening, worship services, and family dinners. If the survivor can get out and spend time with others rather than being alone, the holidays will be a much happier time.

76

Give the family a Christmas ornament in memory of the deceased.

This is a beautiful tribute to the deceased and a wonderful reminder for the family. There is a variety of ideas that you could use for this. You could make an ornament by taking a plain glass ball, writing the name of the deceased on it in glue, and then rolling the glued area in glitter. Blow the excess glitter away, and you have a simple yet lovely tribute to the deceased. If you are not the arts and crafts type, card shops offer a variety of cards and ornaments that you can use. Maybe the deceased had a favorite animal or pastime, and you are able to find that captured on an ornament. There are many ornaments that have the year printed on them if you wish. You will find ornaments of ceramic, glass, plastic, and wood; ornaments from movies, from children's shows, and of commercial products; animal ornaments, ornaments that light up, ornaments that move, and ornaments that have sound. There is such a wonderful selection that there just has to be one out there to capture the memory of the deceased for the Christmas holiday.

If the family does not celebrate Christmas, there are plenty of other items available for holidays that the family does celebrate. For a Jewish family, for example, you could find a kiddush cup or a Menorah with a personal touch to be used each year. Be creative and have fun. Yes, I said have fun. Remembering someone is fun; let the warm memories and happy thoughts help you find your own special way of including the deceased in the holidays this year and every year to follow.

77

Do not ignore the fact that one more chair is empty this year.

Maybe the place at the table is not set, but in the survivors' hearts, there is an empty metaphorical chair that cannot be filled. Do not be afraid to acknowledge this. There is nothing wrong with saying, "It sure feels different this year," or "I really miss Grandma's special stuffing." Chances are you are not the only one thinking about this. Bringing it up breaks the tension that some may be feeling, and it opens the conversation to memories and good times from holidays past.

Often people go through the dinner, the day, or even the entire holiday period full of emotions and memories that they are afraid to share. In order to avoid a painful topic, everyone seems to put those thoughts on the back burner and keep them to themselves. This can be another cause for holiday blues. Encourage survivors to be open and honest with how they feel and to talk about it when they miss the deceased. Instead of offending anyone or causing sad emotions, the topic is more likely to turn out to be a happy one. Once the others realize that there is nothing wrong with talking about the deceased, stories will begin and probably continue throughout the day.

78

> # Send flowers for the anniversary of the death; the first anniversary is always the most difficult, but each anniversary is a painful reminder.

The first anniversary of the death is rough, plain and simple. The survivor often feels alone, isolated, depressed, and anxious. Generally, the anxiety begins when the month of the anniversary begins, and if the anniversary is late in the month, the tension builds for the entire time. Suddenly, the day has arrived, it occurs, and the next day is one of relief. But during this process, the survivor wonders if he or she is alone, if he or she is the only one who remembers what happened and that it happened on that date. Flowers are one way to express your "remembrances," but a card will do just as well. The important thing here is to recognize the anniversary—to let the survivor know that yes you remember, you are thinking of him or her, and you care. This is not only applicable for the first anniversary but for each one. Each year tends to get a little better because the survivor is learning to cope in his or her own way and learns and grows more each year. This date, however, will never be forgotten in the mind or in the heart of the survivor, and if you can make the effort to recognize this, the individual will appreciate it.

79

Bake a cake on the deceased's birthday and celebrate with the survivor by remembering the fun times.

If you know the favorite flavor of cake or a favorite decoration the deceased enjoyed, bake it up and celebrate with the survivor. The survivor will remember the birthday and probably will be down about the whole day, but if you show up with a cake and a few good memories, it will help turn a sad day into a happy day.

You could even surprise the survivor by blowing up balloons, decorating, and having a birthday remembrance party. The survivor will be thankful that you cared enough to remember and acknowledge the birthday.

80

Help the survivor decorate the grave on Memorial Day.

Many people go out on Memorial Day to decorate graves of loved ones. Even though the cemeteries are filled with people decorating their loved ones graves, no survivor wants to go decorate the alone. In fact, the survivor may be reluctant to do it at all, especially on the first Memorial Day following the death. Again, you can make this an enjoyable day rather than a depressing task. Buy bright, cheery flowers, a grave blanket, or a decoration that suits the deceased. Pack up the car with the decorations and a sack lunch. Don't forget hedge trimmers. You and the survivor will be able to groom and decorate the plot and afterward can eat the lunch together in the cemetery. It provides a peaceful setting.

I have done this on several occasions, and I find that it is actually enjoyable to spend a day planning, grooming, and decorating a grave site and then eating a lunch in the serene cemetery. Friends who have been with me on such occasions also have found it to be a pleasant experience.

81

Purchase a memory candle for the survivor to be burned on the deceased's birthday, anniversary, or any other special holiday.

A memorial candle can be wonderful and comforting. I once wrote a letter to a friend who had suffered the sudden death of his sister shortly before Thanksgiving. I enclosed the candle and told him in the letter that the candle was to be lit when he felt that it was appropriate (e.g., her birthday, Christmas, the anniversary of her death, and any other holiday he wanted to light it to represent her). I also mentioned to him that it could be a family event or a personal event for him to do alone, and it was to be lit when he decided it should be. His mother read this letter and told him that she wanted a candle, too, so she could do the same. My friend was not able to light the candle for the Christmas holiday, but in March, for her birthday, he went home and lit it for that evening. He felt sad and emotional, but the next day he told me that he also felt relieved, that he was comforted with the soft glow and the light that represented her. It brought him a sense of peace. I realized then that this was the perfect gift for someone who is grieving and needs a special "light" of hope, love, and peace.

In this particular situation, I bought a candle that was pink because that was the deceased's favorite color. You may want to customize it in some way too. I also bought a candle holder so that new candles could be purchased and the memory tradition could continue. There are a lot of options for you here, so be creative and make it a special, unique tribute to the deceased.

GIFTS

82

Make a donation to the charity of the family's choice in memory of the deceased.

If you know of a charity or group that the family of the deceased supports, make a donation in memory of the deceased. It is such a nice tribute, and the family will appreciate it. Maybe the family's church or other place of worship has special groups such as those that help the needy, a youth group, a scripture study group, a coffee hour after worship, or even an opportunity to provide flowers for an upcoming service. The place of worship is always a good place to start because the members know the deceased's family, and it will give them each an opportunity to approach the family and offer condolences or inquire as to how the family is doing.

If the deceased suffered from a disease or if another member of the family is suffering from an illness, look for a charity for that particular ailment. There are nonprofit organizations that thrive on donations such as this, and you can find many listed in the phone book can or ask around.

There also may be a special group that the family and the deceased supported in their town. The deceased could have been a member of a club or group, participated in a haunted house every year, or volunteered for a community service organization. Because there are so many options, you can take a good look around and do something personal and meaningful for the family in memory of the deceased.

83

If there is no charity designated by the family, give to one of your choice and let the family know.

If you have a difficult time finding a charity that the family supports and you feel uncomfortable asking the survivors, choose one yourself. Maybe you are active in a group and you would like to honor the deceased by donating to that group. Go ahead, and let the family know what you have done. They will appreciate the thought, and they will enjoy the fact that the money is going to a group that you believe in.

84

| Plant a tree in memory of the deceased. |

Planting a tree is a beautiful honor for the deceased. This is also an event that can grow into a tradition. A woman once told me that she purchases a tree for a friend each year on the anniversary of her son's death. She chose a tree that blooms at that time of year, and when she presents one to a friend, she tells that friend why she is doing this for him or her. She said that she likes to do nice things for others, and this makes her feel good and feel at peace with her infant son's death. She wanted something good to come from her sadness, and now instead of feeling sorrow each year at the anniversary of his death, she looks forward to sharing nature. It is a memorial that continues to provide enjoyment to each person, and it is good for the environment too.

85

Give a tree to the family for their yard; include a memory plaque if possible.

If the previous suggestion appeals to you, you could purchase a tree for the family's yard the first year and then continue to buy trees for friends and family each year following. It is nice to include the family in this first, though. You could give them a gift certificate, choose the tree yourself, or make an afternoon out of it by taking the survivor out to find a tree that he or she likes.

If you want to include an additional memorial with the tree, purchase a plaque with the name of the deceased and the date if you so desire, and mount it on a little stand in front of the tree in the family's yard. Survivors truly appreciate this. For a deceased adult, it is a tribute. In the case of a deceased child, it allows the family to watch the tree grow through the years in place of the child. It is comforting.

**Buy an inspirational book for the adult
survivor. Books about near-death
experiences, angels, death,
and healing often are good choices.**

Survivors sometimes find comfort in reading about death or the spiritual world. Books on these topics often offer a peaceful vision of death and the after life or even about angels that may be guiding us as we live our lives. Regardless of what your or the survivor's spiritual beliefs are, these books can be interesting and comforting.

Near-death experiences are nice to read about because most people who have them talk about beautiful places and peaceful feelings, and a wonderful place beyond to which they would like to return. Some say that they did not even want to "come back to life" but were guided to do so. What a relief to read about this and think that maybe the deceased went on to a place such as these that are described.

It also may be reassuring to read about angels and people who have had "experiences" with angels. Some survivors believe that their loved ones are now guardian angels for them or their families. Others believe that angels are protecting the deceased. There are various theories and thoughts on the subject, and I believe that whatever thought comforts the survivor, that is the one to support.

Books about healing come in various forms. Some will tell the story of someone who has gone through a trauma and survived. These books also will explain how the survivor made it through the tough times. You probably will be able to find a book dealing specifically with the situation the survivor with whom you are working has gone through (e.g., death from illness, miscarriage, suicide, old age, homicide, etc.). There are books on the market today addressing seemingly every possibility. Other healing books will be more general, perhaps including a series of short stories or a step-by-step guide to coping. You know the survivor and the situation, so choose a book accordingly that will both help and comfort the survivor.

Another nice idea is to find an inspirational book or calendar with daily meditations of love and support. This is a wonderful gift that the survivor will look forward to reading daily.

Different people have different beliefs. Support the survivor in his or her own beliefs, so long as they provide comfort. There are many books available on these subjects. Search out your local book store and ask for assistance.

87

Send a plant to the funeral home rather than cut flowers. Flowers die, but plants survive as a memorial to the deceased.

Why suffer more death? It can be depressing to watch flowers wilt and die over the couple of weeks following the funeral, and then the survivor has to throw the flowers out and go through a sense of loss (relating to the original loss) all over again. Let the plant live on as a memorial for a family member. The survivors can take these plants home, care for them, and use them to represent the deceased. It is nice for the family to receive several plants from individuals so that each family member is able to take one home. Do not feel that if others have sent plants, yours will not be appreciated. It will be.

I still have a plant given to my family when my grandfather died, and I water it and care for it and it makes me happy. This plant is a pleasant reminder to me of what a wonderful man he was, and something that resulted from his death lives on. I see the new growth and the rich green leaves flourish, and I see that life goes on around us. It is a beautiful reminder for me that is also good for the environment.

88

Purchase a nice frame for a photo
of the deceased.

There is nothing wrong with having pictures of the deceased on display. Some people believe that it is inappropriate to do so, but the truth usually is quite the contrary. When a person dies, the memories and good times do not die with him or her. Pictures are based on memories that the survivor and the deceased have made together, and those memories need to live on. Find a nice frame for the survivor, and if you have a picture of the deceased, include it with the frame. Encourage the survivor to hang it out in the open for others to see.

I knew a family that went even beyond this idea. The family moved to a new home after the death of a child. The child had been ill and the parents knew that the problems were terminal, but they cherished every moment they had with the child. In their new home, they decorated a bedroom with this child's pictures and other little reminders. It was a nursery of sorts that provided the family with a haven of warmth and of memories. They had beautiful baby frames with pastel colors and animals around the borders. This family went to great lengths to decorate and preserve the memories of the baby with pictures, and it was a beautiful tribute.

Many families do not have the space required to keep a single room in the house as a memorial to the deceased, and for some families this could be too emotionally difficult. This is why it is nice to give the gift of a frame for a memento of the deceased that the family can share with all who visit.

89

Give the survivor a blank book
to use as a writing journal.

This is a healthy, creative outlet and a way to track the individual's day-to-day feelings. This is a personal journal, though, and you should not expect the individual to share this intimate look at his or her feelings with you or anyone else. There will be very special, personal items recorded here, items that the survivor may not feel comfortable sharing with anyone. The idea of the journal is to give the individual the opportunity to confide in a book everything that he or she is not willing to share with others. It even may give the survivor the chance to do some soul searching and sort through some confusing elements of his or her life. Writing may help sort out the emotions and feelings of grief, and the individual can look back and reflect on earlier thoughts. On bad days, the survivor can reread the good days, and he or she will have an opportunity to truly "let it all out" without feeling like a burden to anyone else.

CRYING

90

Cry with the survivors.

Do not feel that you need to be strong and set an example for the survivors by not crying. If you feel the urge to cry, do it! Do not be ashamed or insecure about letting your emotions show and crying with the survivor. This most likely will not make the survivor feel worse; in fact, it probably will lend a sense of normalcy to the feelings that the survivor is experiencing. While working with children at a grief center, I found that they were much more comfortable crying and talking to me through their tears if I cried too. This allowed them to feel as if they truly were relating to me, as if I knew what they were going through and felt the pain that they were feeling. When I did not cry, they seemed to feel hindered. They seemed to believe that if they cried it would make them weak and cry-babyish, and children often do not want to appear this way. Adults are similar. Adults want to have their feelings validated. If you cry when you feel you need to, they feel that it is acceptable for them to cry. No one ever should be ashamed of showing true feelings, especially while grieving.

91

Convince survivors that
it is acceptable to cry.

Survivors often believe that they should not cry in public and should be strong instead. Crying is natural and healthy, and pride should be no good reason to prevent oneself from crying. Crying is not a sign of weakness or despair, but rather an outlet for emotions. Help the survivors realize this, but do not force the issue. If the individual is not ready to cry, that is fine too. People grieve at different paces. Everyone sheds tears at some time, and each person has a different breaking point at which he or she no longer can hide the emotions or tears that have been building inside. If you see that the survivor is fighting back the tears and you feel that it is because he or she does not want to lose composure in front of you, reassure the individual that you are fine with his or her tears and that it is acceptable to cry. You may want to have tissues handy when you visit the survivor during the first few months following the death. You may think that the individual is all cried out but then may be amazed by how long the emotional grieving can last. Be patient and remember that there is no limit on tears or sadness. There also is no limit on patience and friendship. Be there and be strong for the person in need.

WHILE AT THE
FUNERAL HOME

92

Visit the funeral home; stay for a while if time permits.

At the funeral home, people constantly are flowing in and out. You may not have much of a chance to visit with the survivors, but they will remember that you were there for them. They appreciate the support of friends and family. It can be difficult to visit the funeral home. It can be uncomfortable and uneasy, and the survivors recognize this. They probably are uncomfortable and uneasy as well. This is a difficult time for everyone involved. If there is a lull in the flow of visitors while you are at the funeral home, make an effort to stay for a while and talk to the survivors if you are able.

If you are very close to the family, you may want to stay to help greet people. When the facility becomes crowded, people sometimes feel intimidated, especially when they cannot speak immediately with the survivor whom they came to see. The longer they wait, the more uncomfortable they become, and they may choose to leave before visiting with the survivor. If you know the visitors and you feel comfortable doing so, go ahead and greet them and visit for a while. It is easier to stand next to a familiar face and chat than to stand alone and feel uncomfortable. You will feel better having someone to talk to, the visitor will be more relaxed and apt to stay longer to visit with the survivor, and the survivor will appreciate your consideration.

93

Bring tissues with you; share them with others who are hurting.

Before leaving for the funeral home or the funeral, grab a few travel packs of tissues. Have them ready and available for anyone who may have forgotten to bring some or for those who run out. Be generous and give tissues to others before the tears start flowing, especially if you notice someone is having a difficult time and is on the verge of crying.

If you forget to bring tissues or if you run out, seek out a funeral director or a church assistant and inquire where you can get more. Most funeral homes and churches will have tissues readily available for these situations. This plan is much nicer than running to the bathroom and bringing along an eight-foot piece of toilet paper to section off to those around you.

FEELINGS OF SURVIVORS

94

Anger, confusion, and pain are all natural feelings following a death.

There are so many stages of grief, and people react differently in each situation. You should be able to differentiate between the stages and help the survivor through each.

Survivors get angry at a variety of items. There may be anger toward the person who died: Why did he or she die? Why would he or she have abandoned the survivor? Why was it his or her time to die? These are all normal questions. Survivors may be angry at others, including a doctor who could not save the deceased, the person who delivered the news of the death, the driver of the car that killed the deceased, or at themselves for not being there to "save" the person. There can be a great deal of anger and a variety of reasons for this anger. Let the survivor be angry and get it out of his or her system, but make sure that the survivor finds a healthy outlet for this anger.

Confusion is another phase of grief. Death of a loved one is a confusing time for everyone. There is so much activity and so many questions that life can become overwhelming for the survivor. The individual may not know if he or she is coming or going. That is where you come in. Help guide the individual. Help with anything that you are able to without getting in the way. Help the individual keep everything together until the major confusion passes.

Pain. The word says it all. If you can sum up experiencing a death in a word, this is probably the word. There is so much pain involved with a loss. The survivor has lost a part of himself or herself—a valuable part that he or she will miss greatly. While there is not much that you can do to make the survivor forget the pain, you can be a friend and be patient until the pain begins to subside. Pain is natural, and you cannot rush the process. Just stick it out and help ease the pain by being there for the survivor when he or she needs you. This is all that you can do.

95

Rage, denial, and fear also are natural feelings following a death.

Rage is similar to anger, but it is an outwardly stronger emotion. Rage is more physical and intense. Rage needs a physical outlet. If the survivor is a physically active person, take him or her out to do something physical. Perhaps the two of you could go to a driving range, batting cage, jogging course, swimming pool, basketball court, tennis court, or racquetball court. Spend an afternoon involved in this activity. If the individual is not an athletic person, find a mutually pleasing activity to burn up energy. Be creative, and find something fun to take the survivor's mind off the death and expel energy at the same time.

Denial is a common feeling as well. Survivors may deny many things. Initially, they may deny the death itself. They may deny their emotions and feelings regarding the death. They even may deny that they are hurting or that they could use a friend to help them through the tough times. Survivors sometimes think that they can make it on their own and that they are supposed to cope without assistance. Recognize this and be patient.

Fear can result from a variety of factors. Especially in small children, it is common for the survivor to fear that he or she as a witness to and survivor of a death will die shortly. Death is scary because it is the "unknown." Try to understand where these fears are coming from. Reassure survivors that life goes on and that we have to enjoy life while we have the opportunity. If we let our fears take over our lives, we will not really *live*. We only will *exist*. While fear is natural, so is life. Keep on going!

96

Reassure the survivor that various feelings are normal.

Survivors may become overloaded with the flood of all of these emotions. It may be difficult to sort out and understand these feelings. The survivor may have many thoughts going through his or her head and may have difficulty sleeping, which only complicates the situation. What the survivor needs is reassurance from you that this is normal, that confusion and frustration are emotions that everyone experiences with a death, and that this all will pass with time.

There are no abnormal feelings when it comes to grieving. No one is new to the emotions or confusion of grief, but each person goes through these stages in a different way and each person tends to think that he or she is the only one ever to feel this way. The survivor also may feel that his or her emotions mean that something is wrong. Often, as the feelings drag on or even progress, the person feels as if life should be getting better and that something is wrong because it seemingly is not getting better. Things will get better, and it will get easier. Just continue to reassure the individual and be supportive.

97

Have a pillow fight; let the survivor release aggressive feelings on the pillow.

A pillow fight is a great physical outlet for the survivor. This is a fantastic activity for small children up through adults. It is a healthy form of acting out. But also realize that the pillow fight does not have to be sad or revolve around the deceased to be a success.

A small child may want to play with a big pillow, wrestle with it, roll around on the floor with it, and maybe even punch and kick it. If you are fortunate enough to have a large punching bag available, the child even may want you to hold it so that he or she can run and attack it or even karate kick it while you brace it. The child is releasing energy and acting out positively. This is a great outlet for a child who is keeping his or her feelings about the death bottled up. It is an opportunity to explode and let loose on a pillow or punching bag.

Teens also enjoy this activity, but they may want to be alone with a punching bag or have friends over to pillow fight. It is an opportunity to get crazy and throw some punches without hurting anyone, including themselves.

For an adult friend, go one on one and have a pillow fight, no holds barred. By the time it is over, you both may be laughing or crying. Either way, it is a physical and emotional release in a safe, controlled environment.

98

Take the survivor to an open field and have a screaming contest. Yell to release the anger.

Take the survivor out into the country and find a quiet place away from people. Have a yelling contest. Just scream out shrills or yell out questions. Encourage the survivor to let it all out. Ask, "Why me?" or "Why does this hurt?" or exclaim, "I am angry!" Yell at each other or just yell together, but let that anger out. You can assist by encouraging the survivor to scream out whatever he or she desires.

The survivor could walk away absolutely exhausted or with a really sore throat, but rest will cure both these ailments. The good news is that the screaming just might help cure the blues and the frustrations that have been building up inside of the survivor. Yelling gives the individual the opportunity literally to explode and let it all out.

If a nearby open field is unavailable, take the survivor into the basement of a home or give the survivor a pillow to yell into. It will muffle the sounds but still allow the survivor to scream and really let loose.

SUPPORT

99

Look into local grief support groups. Attend with the survivor if you are able.

Support groups can be very valuable for the entire family and even friends of the deceased. Look through your local paper or yellow pages to find what is available in your area. Call for information on the group and to see if there are any openings or if you need to reserve a spot.

When attending, remember that all of your problems will not be solved in an evening. Support groups are for support, and some people need more attention than others on certain days. It is a give-and-take atmosphere, and individuals need to take their turn and then offer support to the others. Some individuals will take months to open up; others will let it all out on the first night. People do not grieve in the same manner or within the same time frame. Be patient, and give it time. Success takes work, effort, and patience. Remember to work on all three.

100

Do not interrupt when a survivor begins to talk about the death.

Once the survivor trusts you enough to open up and discuss his or her feelings, do not interrupt. Let the survivor go with it. Your interruptions may signal to the survivor that he or she is rambling on, that this discussion is not welcomed, or that you are bored with what he or she has to say. It may take a long time for the individual to open up or feel comfortable talking about the death, so do not hinder the progress that has been made. Let the survivor just run with his or her thoughts, pause, think, and ask you questions. Join the conversation when asked to, but listen until that point. You may find that once the individual begins talking, there will be no stopping until he or she gets it all out. This is healthy, so be supportive and let him or her take the floor.

101

Allow long pauses for the individual to collect his or her thoughts on what to say next.

Pauses are just that: pauses. Individuals put their thoughts into paragraphs almost, and they sometimes need to pause between each one to take a breath before going on to the next area. Respect these preparatory pauses, and allow the individual to utilize them. Sometimes the individual may begin to feel emotional but may not be ready to cry. The survivor may want to get all of the conversation out of the way before the emotions begin to pour forth. Allow for this so that the individual can go at his or her own pace and format for discussion.

SILENCE AND PATIENCE

102

Never assume that the silence needs to be broken.

The old saying is true: "Silence is golden." Silence is not meant to be broken; it is a time to collect thoughts, to review what has been said already, and to take a break to catch a breath. If you jump in and interrupt, you may throw the individual off track and hamper his or her talking to you.

There may be times when you can use silence as a tool to direct the conversation in a particular fashion. For example, you may want to make a statement to introduce a new topic, but to get the survivor to respond you need to leave a window of silence that is to be broken by the him or her. If you want to talk about the pain of the loss, you could state, "Boy, there sure is a lot of pain involved in death and grief." Then wait, silently, and the survivor will have to break the silence. It may take a while, but wait for the response. This gives you the opportunity to bring up a topic that you want to discuss, and it gives the survivor an opportunity to approach the topic the way he or she prefers. Silence is a wonderful tool.

103

> ## Do not feel insulted if the survivor does not turn to you right away. Give the individual time.

You may be the survivor's best friend ever, but he or she may not want to turn to you right away. The survivor may want to recluse and put off discussing this for a while. Keep in mind, though, that the survivor will come around, and he or she will need you to be there when the time comes.

104

Be patient.

Patience is so important when dealing with death and grief. You may feel that the survivor is not progressing at the rate he or she should, or you may think that the individual is not getting on with life. This is not your decision to make. You need to understand that each individual grieves differently, and if you want to help and want to be a friend through this, you need to be patient and understanding. Most importantly of all, you cannot be judgmental.

GENERAL SUGGESTIONS

105

Recognize that the survivors are continuing to suffer.

Suffering does not end when the deceased has died. Survivors will continue to suffer long after. There may be feelings of guilt due to watching the deceased suffer from an ailment such as a stroke, a brain tumor, cancer, lupus, multiple sclerosis, etc. These diseases are debilitating and horrible to witness. Although there is nothing a survivor can do other than make the suffering individual comfortable, the survivor wishes that he or she could have done something more.

Even if the deceased did not suffer from a debilitating disease or injury, the survivors still will suffer themselves. Especially in the case of a "quick" death such as the result of an automobile accident or a heart attack, the survivors hope that the deceased did not suffer and wonder if he or she did. In some ways, these survivors suffer to a greater extent. They were not prepared for the death and did not have an opportunity to say good-bye, whereas in the case of a disease, survivors often will have said their good-byes after each visit as if anticipating that it will be the last time together.

106

> ## Do not force the survivor to talk about his or her feelings. Let the individual open up to you at his or her own pace.

This can take days, months, or even years. One time frame is not necessarily better than another. Some individuals want to let it all out right now, no hesitation. This is less frustrating for you as a listener and friend because you are able to help almost immediately and you feel a sense of accomplishment. Do not force this, however. If the person wants to open up, he or she will.

Sometimes it may take a while. The survivor needs time to think, to collect his or her thoughts, and to figure out how he or she really feels about the entire scope of issues. The survivor may come to you when you least expect it, maybe months down the road, and just let it all out with everything from discussing feelings to sobbing for hours. Be patient and be supportive.

And then there is the delayed griever. Sometimes people use avoidance to get themselves through feelings that they want to deny. Then, out of the blue, they are ready to grieve years later and long after everyone else has passed this point. I know a couple who lost a child in the final month of pregnancy. The mother grieved immediately and, although it took years, she accepted the loss, dealt with the feelings, and became all right with it. The father, on the other hand, denied the loss and denied his feelings for nearly 20 years. Suddenly, he began to grieve and wanted to acknowledge the loss by talking about it and visiting the grave. Imagine dealing with a death 20 years after it has occurred. But this is how grief is—it is different for each person, and you cannot predict how it will affect each survivor. So instead of predicting, put your energies into supporting.

107

> **Never assume that any amount of time
> is enough to "forget" a death.
> Loved ones always remember.**

No holiday ever will be the same, no family outing ever will be held without a thought of the deceased. The loved ones may not always cry or outwardly grieve over the loss because with time it does get easier, but there always will be a sense of loss and a sense that someone is missing.

108

> ## Keep in mind that the person died, but the memories did not.

Survivors do not forget the deceased or the events in the life that the deceased led. Only the physical being of the person is gone. The good times and even the bad times are still there. Survivors still may hear songs that remind them of special times with the deceased, they may see someone who looks like or walks like or talks like the deceased, or they may run into friends of the deceased. There are constant reminders, and these reminders are not going to vanish given any amount of time. Respect this, and do not try to convince the survivor that these reminders are meaningless, silly, or unhealthy. Reminders allow the deceased to live on in our minds. It is healthy to miss someone and to want to be reminded of someone. It may appear as if the survivor is looking for reminders; he or she should be free to do so. If that is this particular survivor's way of dealing with the death, then so be it. Remember, we all grieve differently. Just because someone does not grieve the way we would like does not make his or her way the wrong way.

109

Remember that our lives continue.

Our lives continue even through we have experienced a death, and we have to go on.

110

Celebrate every day you have as if it is your last; life is unpredictable.

INDEX

(Index reflects item numbers, 1 through 110)

ABOUT THE AUTHOR

Emily Waszak is a motivational speaker with programs primarily focusing on self-esteem. The author's interest in grief and comfort began when she volunteered at a grief center for children. While meeting several families and hearing their stories, she realized there was a need for a guide to grieving, and her quest began. She also has been published in several books and magazines for her poetry and articles on various topics including grief work.

Waszak attended Michigan State University and earned a B.A. in English–Creative Writing. She resides in Michigan with her husband, Jeremy, and a menagerie of pets.